STRESS-FREE RETIREMENT

*Living the Millionaire Life
After Retirement*

I0485491

FHILCAR FAUNILLAN

Table of Contents

Introduction

I would like to extend my warmest gratitude for buying this book entitled, *"Stress-Free Retirement: Living the Millionaire Life After Retirement."*

This book contains many helpful information about one of the most important milestones in anyone's life, and that is no other than - **retirement**.

What is retirement? In general, we can describe retirement as the time when you reap the benefits of all your life's work for which a lot of people are looking forward to enjoying it. And I know that many of you have been curious about this especially those who are already planning to retire and spend the rest of their lives comfortably and leisurely.

Get to know the most important things about retirement in Chapter 1, from its various benefits to the aspects that make it perfect and complete. It will shed light on all the speculations and myths that surround this topic. In Chapter 2, you will know your retirement options - whether to avail it earlier in your life or perhaps a little later as well as doing it overseas or domestically. You'll find some valuable advice as to the perfect time to retire in Chapter 3, including the signs that serve as a signal that you may be ready to retire. Chapter 4 will be your guide in making your retirement plan. And finally, Chapter 5 will give you several suggestions on how to spend your time when you retire, including the activities that you can enjoy as well as fun-filled yet straightforward money-making ideas. Discover all these as you read through each chapter.

I hope you'll enjoy it

CHAPTER 1

Things You Should Know First

About Retirement

Everyone must have dreamed of reaching this point in their lives. Retirement - it's such a wonderful phase in anyone's life, isn't it?

While some people end up living for their work, most of us work to live, and the endgame for all these toils is finally experiencing the fruits of our labor and enjoying our lives without having to stress ourselves and wake up to spend However, retirement may not be the ultimate dream for some people, as in some cases, they might have been forced to retire due to health reasons or perhaps because the law so requires. Even so, we all must stop working at some point in our lives, whether we need it or not. So, starting from this chapter up to the end of this book, you will learn about how to have a stress-free retirement and at the same time, live like a millionaire. By "living the millionaire life", I do not mean that you need to have millions on your bank accounts. What is meant by this line is being happy and contented in having everything you need. Whether you want to retire by choice or not, there are still many advantages that you can enjoy from it.

The Benefits of Retirement

1. **Having more time to do the things that you love.** With lots of free time, come lots of possibilities. Retirement can be the perfect opportunity for you to find new hobbies or try out things and activities you have always wanted to do. You can spend this time learning about new stuff and set new goals and priorities. Most retirees try on many hobbies or study about subject matters that

they are curious about. Travelling is also a way by which retirees can spend much of their time.

2. **No more stress.** Many studies conducted over the years have already showed that one's occupation is one of the significant sources of stress. Recall the times when you had to scurry off for work, almost had a heart attack because of traffic, constantly endure the pressure your boss has given you, always had to deal with difficult colleagues and clients, and went home tired and barely able to have time for yourself and your family. During your employment, you had to go through all these stresses every single day. When you retire, you are putting an end to all these hassles. Well, retirement does not offer a complete absence of pressure. However, you surely will notice a significant decrease in your stress levels once you retire. Imagine sleeping early each day and waking up late in the morning without worrying about the consequences like getting flak from your boss and having your salary deducted. All you must worry about is how to spend your day,

what to eat for dinner, and where to go to have your next vacation, and things like that.

3. **Having much time to take care of your health.** In connection with stress, being employed is also one of the main reasons why people are not able to properly pay attention to their health, causing ailments to further complicate especially in one's later years where a person's immune system slowly weakens. Retirement can be the perfect remedy to put an end to your life's stress. Once you retire, you will have more time to do worthwhile activities that can greatly contribute to your health like regularly exercising, sleeping for more extended hours, and being able to cook healthful meals.

4. **More time with your family.** As you now own all your time, you can spend this by finally making memorable moments with your family. You will have more time to take vacations with them, spend nice and fun family dinners every day, and take care of your grandchildren if any. Retirement is also the opportunity to reconnect with your family members and relatives, even your

friends, whom you haven't contacted with for years.

5. **Social work and helping the community.** You can also become a helpful and outstanding member of your community. Most people retire when they are already in their later years, a time when they have saved enough money for leisure and when they have a lot of free time to spare. At this stage in your life, you can find a more sensible and productive use of your resources by contributing to society.

Myths about Retirement

Before you proceed, there are a lot of things about retirement that should be made clear for you to understand it better and be able to make the right decisions. Enlighten yourself with the most common retirement myths.

a) **The Comprehensive Health Insurance**

It has become a regular practice for retirees to rely on their health insurances for their health care needs for the rest of their retirement. However, health insurances cannot guarantee that all your health needs throughout your retirement will be covered. While it is true that these health insurances can help much in shouldering the costs of your regular checkups and hospital bills, the same can be limited. Most health insurances do not cover long-term care or custodial care, as well as fees for dental care and the like. Moreover, though most insurance plans like these include the cost of an item or service, there are still fees that you need to pay such as your coinsurance, copayments, and deductibles. That is why you must plan your retirement health savings to fit your needs and not just rely on these insurance plans.

b) **The Golden Figure**

While many people usually establish a specific savings goal by picking a target number out of the blue and deciding right there that it would be their goal, some base theirs on figures which are provided by so-called retirement experts. Unfortunately, setting your savings goals without proper planning and analysis on your own is not the best way to go about things.

There is no established savings amount that you can merely make as your savings goal. It all depends on your situation. In setting up your target savings for your retirement, try to consider different aspects of your finances such as your present income, bank balance, job stability, future financial projections, plans, and such.

People also believe that by withdrawing only a certain percentage from their savings for retirement every year that will not cause much of a decrease in their savings. Some sources establish a specific amount like 3% to 5%, and unfortunately, people follow suit. Just like in setting up your savings goal, there is no definite number for your rate of withdrawal. You must consider your current and future conditions before setting up any plan.

Besides, you always have the choice of changing your targets as your circumstances change.

c) Lesser Tax Payments

One of the things that most retirees expect during their retirement is paying lesser tax. However, this is not entirely true. While there is a chance for that, the same is only true if your income is lesser too. If you still earn as much as when you were working, then you are more likely to pay the same tax. Plus, there is also a chance that tax rates may increase by the time you retire.

d) The Unsecured Social Security

You would think that social security will not do a bit much for your retirement since most people think of it as unsecured and insufficient to cover all your retirement costs. But then social security is not meant to shoulder every aspect of your expenses throughout your retirement. Despite this, experts consider social security as one of the most stable ways of funding your retirement. Through careful planning and estimation, you can build up your future benefits to a higher amount and foresee how much you will benefit for your retirement.

e) Lesser Spending in Retirement

A most common misconception about retirement spending is that it will be significantly lower than before retirement. Many have claimed that retirees spend 20% to 30% less compared to that when they were still employed. However, as reiterated continuously in this chapter, every person's circumstances differ. Your spending rate and pattern will change depending on how you plan to spend the rest of your retirement. You may plan to travel all the time or decide to tackle on new and perhaps, costly endeavors.

f) Work Dependence

While it is a good thing to keep yourself busy during your retirement and generate enough income to cover some expenses, mainly relying on work to sustain yourself (and perhaps your family) is not a good idea. Other than defeating the primary purpose of retirement plans, it is also very unreliable. Most retirees retire at a later age where the body is not as healthy as it was to handle stress from work, and besides, it's rare to find a job that accepts retirees.

What Makes Up For A Perfect Retirement?

Now that you have been clarified of the previous topics, you must be curious about what makes an ideal retirement. Although each retiree has different needs and goals in their retirement, the following elements are needed if you want to be secure and have the best time for the rest of your life.

- ***Enough money***. Money may not be everything there is to life, but it is one need which you cannot wholly shun. Whether you like it or not, having the money or at least a source of finances for your retirement is the most vital to living comfortably and securely.

Most importantly, it helps you do the things you want to do. Besides, isn't this one of the primary reasons why you were working hard in the first place?

- **Clear purpose**. If you ask retirees what their most common apprehensions are, their answer would probably be having a reason to wake up each morning. We devote much of our time working to provide for ourselves and even our families. Waking up every day and going to work has become a daily routine for most people, that on the day of their retirement, they are jarred. It seems that one is trying to learn how to live again. That is why experts believe that the best retirement is characterized by having a purpose. Do an activity that will give you personal satisfaction, something that will make you proud of doing it, something with relevance and significance. You may want to volunteer in your community and share your knowledge, join a non-profit organization, write a book, donate, and more.

- **Better health**. Forget the image of a satisfied old person in a wheelchair knitting or staring at the sunset. While you may inevitably come to that point in your life, it is not how the entirety of your retirement should be. A perfect retirement translates to having better health and being fit to be able to do the things you have always wanted. They say that life is unfair during old age as you might have all the time and the money in the world, but none of your original energy left to spend them. Well, with the recent advances in health and medicine, this statement is bound to become weaker. Start taking care of your health and well-being right now, and you will be one step nearer to the retirement experience of your dreams.

- **Enough ties**. Just as it is jarring to one day wake up and find no purpose in getting out of bed, waking up and realizing that you have kept your family and loved ones at a distance is also worrying. Throughout the years that you spent working, you may have had lost touch with friends and relatives, or parted ways with partners and spouses. This is now the time to rekindle your ties and spend more time reconnecting with your family. It is ideal that you have someone to wake up for every day, to cap off the perfect retirement.

CHAPTER 2

Options for Retirement

Before making your retirement plans, there are many options that you might want to consider. This chapter will introduce you to these options along with its pros and cons. Remember that some of these options might not suit you well, so be careful in considering them. Learn about these options below.

Early, Normal or Late Retirement?

The choice of early, normal or late retirement

depends widely on many factors, and the suitability of each option most likely varies from person to person. To help you decide, read through each option's advantages and disadvantages. But before going through those, you must first understand what differentiates them from each other.

Early retirement is defined as ending one's employment before the retirement age set forth by law or contract. Most people consider retiring at the age of 55 or earlier than 50 while others peg it at any age before 65. Normal retirement, on the other hand, is stopping working at an age where one can already receive the most benefits he can get, that is, the age set by law or the institution you are working for. In the United States, 67 is considered the normal retirement age while around the world, it can be as early as 60. Late retirement, consequently, is quitting the workforce later than the normal retirement age.

Early Retirement
Advantages

Retiring early gives you more time to do the activities you desire. Through early retirement, you can travel more, have more time with your loved ones, engage in more hobbies, and have enough energy to enjoy.

There are a lot of retirees that plan to start their own business during retirement. If you plan to be one of these like-minded businessmen, then early retirement is perfect for you. Putting up your own business is not something you can dive into without preparation. The sooner you can start your business, the earlier it is for you to overcome the roadblocks and enjoy its benefits.

The earlier you let go of the stressful lifestyle brought about by work, the better it is for your health. Getting an early breather is beneficial for you, especially when you are engaged in both physically and mentally taxing work. By retiring early, you can also have more time to focus on your health and participate in programs that ensure longevity.

The inevitability of death always looms around the corner, and this is even more pronounced in a person's later years. A weakened immune system and poor metabolism become the trigger for a disease-prone body. In addition, accidents also have a more likelihood of occurring. Retiring early makes sure you can enjoy the fruits of your hard work.

Disadvantages

The attractiveness of the benefits that you can get from retirement is proportional to the length of your employment. That is, the earlier you start your retirement, the lesser benefits you will get, may they be from your pension or social security and the likes. This is one known drawback to early retirement.

Years and years of working may have been quite ingrained in your life that a sudden change in your situation might affect you in many ways. Many early retirees have reported experiencing psychological distress during the first few days of retirement, especially those who are known to be hardworking and competitive individuals. A drastic change in one's daily activities and routines may disorient you and getting used to it may take some time.

Another disadvantage of early retirement is having lesser time in saving money for actual retirement. Vis-à-vis the diminution in the benefits that you can receive is also the decrease in your opportunity to save more from your wages. And its impact is more felt especially when you are trying to save for bigger projects, like a house, a lot, or your dream car.

If you are the type of person that makes lasting friendships at work, retiring earlier than your colleagues may be an issue for you. Your time spent with them is the thing that will be most affected. You will have to spend lesser time with them, and that may strain your relationships. Also, while you might find enough time to catch up, your topics of conversation and interests may not jive anymore.

Late Retirement

Advantages

The longer you extend your employment, the longer will be your chances of gathering more resources for your retirement. Prolonged employment may require you to endure the hardships of work and stress for a longer period, but the effort is not for nothing. Think about it, you will have more money to save, but a shorter time to spend them all. You will not have to worry about eventually using up all your savings.

Another advantage of late retirement is the increase in benefits. Pensions are a good example of this. Pensions normally increase in every year that you delay claiming it. The longer you start your retirement and claim your pension, the more increment you can benefit from it.

While staying longer at your job may most likely expose you to most stressors, continuing your occupation for a few more years might be good to keep your mind active and fit. This is true mostly for people with jobs that do not really require too much mental, emotional, or physical effort.

Disadvantages

While early retirement may offer the disadvantage of having a shorter time to build up your funds and savings, late retirement, on the other hand, shortens the time you can spend on your actual retirement. It would be a shame to stop working and find yourself too incapable of doing the activities you originally planned on doing after quitting your occupation.

This might be quite unsettling, but the idea of mortality is one thing that cannot be untwined from the concept of retirement. Death can come to us at any time and the longer we prolong our sought-after rest from decades of work, the higher the chance that we can no longer enjoy it because of accidents and unfortunate illnesses.

This last disadvantage might not affect you as a

retiree, but it concerns the new workforce. It has been found that old employees are more numerous than new younger hires and that the presence of these former employees makes it difficult for the young generation of workers to get employed.

CHAPTER 3

Domestic or Overseas Retirement?

Given enough planning and a clever savings scheme, you can easily have the choice of retiring in your own place and country or abroad. While most would-be retirees prefer to settle down in their country, quite a number look forward to moving abroad to spend their retirement. Some also like to enjoy their time moving from one country to another. Knowing the benefits and drawbacks of each option may help you decide which would be the best for you.

Domestic Retirement

Advantages

When you are old enough, you get used to things, like the brand of shampoo you use, the brand of bread, the restaurant you regularly take your family for dinner, your house, your neighborhood, and such. By choosing domestic retirement, the burden of having to adjust to a new culture and a new way of life can be avoided. You will have the stability and consistency in life, the disruption of which might affect you in negative ways. You can remain to live the way you are most comfortable with.

One good thing about staying in your own country for your retirement is still having ready professional support. You may have past employers and business acquaintances whom to call on if ever you are in financial trouble or might need temporary employment. Connections such as these can only be effectively utilized when you are near them.

Other than staying connected with other people for professional support, being able to keep your friends, family, and acquaintances near is also a huge advantage for domestic retirement. There will always be people to support you if ever you undergo problems. Most domestic retirees find being near their loved ones has helped make their lives easier. In staying in your country, your family will be there to support you, your friends will be there to have fun with you, your grandchildren will be there to cheer you up, and when it comes to emergencies, your loved ones will be just a phone call away.

Disadvantages

Related to the living expense of being in a country like the US, one negative thing to consider is the ever-growing cost of medical care in the country. Recently, it has been reported that a retiree might have to use up at least $100, 000 a year for healthcare expenses.

If you are the type of person who is always looking for an adventure and has always yearned of having new experiences, retiring in your own country might limit your chances of experiencing new things. Also, hindering a change of environment might cost you the benefit of being healthier and happier.

Most disadvantages revolving around staying in the country relates to expenses. The possibility that you might be more financially disadvantaged when you stay in your country than in another is likely. This is more emphasized when you are living in a country like the United States because of the high cost of living.

Overseas Retirement

Advantages

For retirees from most European and American countries, the weather is one strong factor in convincing them of choosing to retire overseas. Most retirees are old people who have health issues that are aggravated by weather and seasonal changes. For example, retirees with arthritis suffer during cold days and the winter season. With overseas retirement, you get to choose a country with a relatively stable climate and unchanging seasons that would be better for your health.

Living in a new country and breathing in a new environment is always exciting. Many retirees who have opted for overseas retirement reported a general increase in their well-being, happiness, and health. This is because most retirement spots provide a more peaceful and nature-centric environment. Besides, a new surrounding encourages new activities that you might not have had done before.

There are countries that most American and European retirees visit because of their very attractive incentive programs for retirees. Of course, you may need to fulfill a few requirements to completely enjoy them. Even so, enjoying an incentive plus a low cost of living is enough to add weight to the option.

Compared to a select few countries like the United States, a lot of countries have a comparably lower cost of living. In these countries, you can easily buy stuff that you may have thought twice buying in your own country. You can thrive in these countries with even just a portion of your savings, maybe even with enough left over to include new endeavors in your retirement plan, like additional vacation or even putting up a small business. Furthermore, healthcare costs are also most likely very affordable in these countries, which is one huge benefit in case a medical problem arises.

Chapter 5 gives you a list of the top 5 best countries where to spend your retirement.

Disadvantages

While staying in another country offers you a chance to experience different activities and a new way of living, it also poses a difficulty in adjusting to the cultural difference. There is the language barrier that would hinder you from socializing with your community, especially when the people do not speak much English. Another thing is the cultural disparity between what you are used to in your own country and your new one. You may have to learn the local customs and practices to avoid any problems with the locals.

Living away from your friends and family could be quite a hassle. Being with them and having their support can be quite difficult when you live countries away. If you want to see them regularly, you might have to shell out quite a lot of money.

Another drawback of overseas retirement is taxation. There are several countries in the world that have different taxation schemes. While some can be advantageous for you, a lot of countries for retirement require you to pay a ridiculous amount of taxes. So, depending on which country you would want to spend the entirety of your retirement in, you may end up paying two taxes every year.

CHAPTER 4

The Perfect Time to Retire

When is the perfect time to retire? This is one of the most important questions that you must answer. While it is common for people to have their retirement date already set out by the government, you have the choice to decide as to when to stop working. If you recall in the previous chapter, you can have the option of retiring early. But again, every person has different circumstances that will determine when the ideal time to retire is. Consider the signs by answering these questions below. If your answer is yes to most of these questions, then you are more than ready to retire.

Preparation for Retirement

a. **Do you have a workplace pension plan?**

Having a workplace pension plan is a sure advantage for you. Presently, only a few employees have applied for a pension plan in the institution they are working for. By having an employer-sponsored plan, you will be able to save through the help of your employer. They will have to invest your contributions, instead of you, so that in the end you will receive your benefits. With this, you can have more retirement confidence, and it can help you not to rely too much on government benefit plans.

b. **Do you already have your own home?**

Do not be quick to say yes just yet. What the question above means is that you have a house that is titled under your name with the mortgage paid off. This is one important thing to consider before retirement. Having a place to stay that you can call your own is imperative for retirees since having a problem with your residence at a point in your life where you are supposed to be doing other things is quite burdening. By owning an already paid off house, you can use the money you are supposed to pay for the house for other uses, like saving for your hobbies, investing, and all that. Plus, you can also use the house to generate more income, which you can add to your emergency funds, or completely live off it.

However, there are also many people discouraging the idea of owning a home, especially when you are already a retiree. According to them, owning a house is much more costly than just renting one. There are maintenance costs and tax payments that come with it, which, for them, are not worth the hassle when you are already old.

c. **Are your children already set in life?**

While you need to keep your connection with your children, you must make sure that they are already independent and can work for themselves. Retirement is the point in a person's life where a parent does not need to provide for their children anymore. In other circumstances, it is even the children themselves that provide for their parents. The important thing here is that you will have minor things to worry about during your retirement. If you are still paying for your children, then it might not yet be the right time for you to stop your employment.

d. **Have you already settled all your debts?**

Having debts is a common problem for people, and any person would know that it is a heavy burden to have for a long time. Before you decide to retire, make sure that you have already taken care of all your debts or any obligations. Start to make a payment scheme to settle everything that you need to settle, like the money you owe to someone, card balances, loans, etc. As a retiree, you are supposed to not worry about debts anymore and just live as unstressed as possible. You are supposed to enjoy every moment, but you cannot do this when you still have those niggling thoughts about your debts. It can only become an unnecessary concern and will spoil the fun of your retirement.

e. **Have you already tried to live like a retiree for a short period of time?**

Retirement is not just any simple event in your life, so it would truly help you if you try to "practice" for it. You must first try living like a retiree by living off a month or two in a retiree's monthly budget. According to experts, a typical retiree has a monthly expense of around $2,500 a month, with almost half of it used for paying your lodging. You can attempt to use only this amount of money in a month. If you manage to comfortably live with this money within that time, then you can probably survive your life as a retiree.

f. **Has your health been affected by your occupation?**

If there is one telltale sign that you should stop working, it is if your work is compromising your health. No matter how set you are about your retirement plans, your health should be the main priorities on deciding when to quit working and start resting. A recent statistical report revealed that less than 50% of would-be retirees followed through their planned retirement date, while others were not able to do so because of unprecedented reasons such as health issues. If you feel that your body is suffering because of your job, it would be wise to terminate your employment. Or if you do not want to retire yet, you can look for a job that will not be much stressful for you.

g. **Have your friends already retired, too?**

As pointed out in the previous chapter, it is important to consider your friends in your retirement decisions. Not being able to retire with your friends together, may be disadvantageous as they can be a form of social support for you during retirement and help you remain active socially. If you are the only one among your group of friends who have not retired yet, it probably is the right time to retire for you. However, it is also good to remember that it is more important that you should go by your own pace and consider your own personal circumstance.

h. **Do you have other channels for generating income other than your job?**

Of course, your job is more important, being your main source of income in the first place. However, to be ready for retirement, you must have at least one other source of income. You can adjust to have a side job, preferably one you can do at home. There are already a lot of income-generating activities that you can do online, like freelance writing and editing jobs, consultancy, and retail selling. If you have a house of your own, you can also rent part of it for additional profit. You should learn to balance your time and try not to overdo yourself, nevertheless. If managed well, these other sources of income can provide a steady source of money for you during the entirety of your retirement.

CHAPTER 5

How to Prepare for Your Retirement

Preparing for your retirement is very important, and one way to get ready for it is to have your own retirement plan. In this chapter, you will be learning all about retirement plans and hcw to proceed in creating your own.

A retirement plan is a program to set up your finances so that you can have enough money in your retirement despite not being employed. Retirement plans can be sponsored by many institutions or bodies. The most common are government-sponsored plans, followed by those sponsored by your employers or the company you are working for. Plans by insurance companies and trade unions are also available. Investing your money is also good to include in your plans.

When you make a retirement plan, you will have to pinpoint your goals for your retirement income, including where you will source them. It also involves dealing with assets, approximating future expenses, and executing a savings plan. In addition to that, you will have to determine whether your expected incomes and savings can reach your retirement goals.

Making a Retirement Plan

1. **Determine where you can source your finances.**

   The following are possible sources of funds that you can utilize:

   a. Social Security

      Whether you are confident with Social Security or not, it is still important to have it. It can provide you with financial support during your retirement. If you already have Social Security, it is advisable that you also register for your own *my Social Security* account online to properly and easily manage it. With this, you can generate estimates for all your future benefits, paid taxes, and records of your earnings. While retiring, you can also easily receive a letter that contains a proof of your benefits.

b. Pensions

Pensions are definite sources of retirement income. There are different pension plans that you can avail of. You can either apply for a pension with your private employer or avail it from the government. Requirements for eligibility may vary, but usually, you need to work for your employer for a specific period and that entail years. And the longer you stay working for your employer, the higher the increase in your benefits will be.

c. An inheritance that you will receive

Inheritances are also a probable source of income in the future. Most inheritances come in the form of real estate properties like lands, houses, and buildings. Cars and other forms of vehicles can be received as inheritances too. You can generate money through these properties by selling them, or you can just rent them off for a sure steady stream of money while you are saving and during your retirement. However, it is also likely that you can also inherit debts, liabilities and other problems that come with these properties, so you need to be careful and manage them well.

d. Other personal properties

Other than real estate properties, you can also generate money from smaller properties like your pieces of jewelry, antique furniture and decor, and rare collections among others. You can sell them to collectors or put them up for auction which will surely grant you a higher price for your possessions.

e. Investment income

Investment is also a sure-fire way of guaranteeing that you can get more from your retirement savings. However, there is a catch. Investing can only be productive if you do it right. Make a wrong move and you will end up in a precarious financial situation. If you haven't already, you should start investing in real estates, bond funds, stock mutual funds, money market funds, and trusts among others. Item no. 4 in this list will help you figure out how to invest wisely.

2. Choose between different retirement plans.

There are many kinds of retirement plans and individual retirement accounts (IRA) out there, but the four of the most common and most important are the following: Traditional IRA, 401 (k) plans, Roth IRA, as well as 403 (b) plans.

a. Traditional IRA

You can get a Traditional IRA from investment houses. Investment houses are usually involved in investment banking and other financial activities, and they can be owned by a single person or a huge organization along with individuals. Visit an investment house so that you can consult with them and set up an account.

For eligibility, you must be working or at least have a spouse that works and have an income. As for age requirements, you just must be younger than 70.5 years to qualify for a traditional IRA.

As for your contributions, you can invest $5,500 every year, and it should not exceed that amount. However, if you are more than 50 years old or will reach that age by the end of the year, you will have to invest at most $6,500. These figures are the currently used rate, which became effective just in 2014 and are significantly higher. The rates might change for the next years to come.

In regard to taxation, a Traditional IRA

enables you to contribute to your account without worrying about paying taxes for it, thus decreasing your bill for your taxes. To cite an example, let us say you have opened a Traditional IRA and is contributing this year $5,500. Next year, when you file for your taxes, you can exclude the $5,500 from your taxable income.

As for the withdrawal period, you will be able to withdraw from your Traditional IRA when you reach 59.5 years old. You can also be free to withdraw during the years after that. However, while you are tax-free before your withdrawal period, you can no longer be tax-free once you start getting money. It will already be considered as your income and so should be included in your tax reports. Of course, you don't have to withdraw right away, but you can only delay getting the money until you become 70 years of age. But if you think about withdrawing earlier than that, do not be discouraged because it is also possible. Earlier withdrawal can be done if you give an additional 10% penalty tax when you withdraw. This may be higher than the standard income tax, but helpful if you really intend to withdraw early, especially when you plan to have an early retirement.

b. Roth IRA

You can get a Roth IRA in the same manner by which you can get a Traditional IRA. You also must go to an investment house or contact one so that you can open an account with them.

As for eligibility, you can avail a Roth IRA with the same requirements as that for a Traditional IRA. If you think you are eligible for the latter, chances are you can also open a Roth IRA.

There are many similarities between a Traditional IRA and a Roth IRA, even the amount that you need to contribute. You still need to invest $6,500 if you are at least 50 years old and $5,500 if you are under that age. However, there are slight limits and conditions in a Roth IRA, depending on your income. If your income is at least $107,000 and at most $122,000 and you are single, you cannot invest more than $5,000 to $6,000 each year. This is also applicable if you have a spouse and your income is at least $169,000 and $179,000 each year. And if your income is above these ranges, you will not be allowed to invest in a Roth IRA.

The real difference between the Traditional IRA and Roth IRA starts with taxation. While a Traditional IRA can only be taxed once you withdraw from it, a Roth IRA is taxable while you are still investing in it. The age for the withdrawal of investment gains is like a Traditional IRA, that is, you can also withdraw when you are already 50.5 years old. Once you reach that age, you will be able to get any amount from your Roth account completely tax-free.

In regard to withdrawal, you can already get money from your account any time you want. That is if you have reached the five-year mark of having the account. However, what you can withdraw at that early period of time is only your contributions, not the gains from your investment. You can only get the fruits of your investment when you reach the specified age of 59.5 years old.

Early withdrawal is also not a problem with a Roth IRA. As stated above, you can withdraw your contributions if you already have that account for at least five years. Once you start withdrawing, you will be able to get money without tax and penalties. However, if you decide to withdraw earlier than the specified 5-year period, you will be given a penalty tax of 10%. The 10% tax penalty is also applied when you withdraw more than your contributions before you reach 59.5 years old, plus taxes.

c. 401 (k) plan and 403 (b) plan

A 401 (k) plan and 403 (b) plan is very similar to each other so they will be discussed as one here. The only thing that separates the two is the nature of the business that you are affiliated with. Basically, the 401 (k) plan is for profit organizations and businesses, while the 403 (b) plan is for non-profit organizations, the government, religious organizations, and schools.

To get a 401 (k) plan or a 403 (b) plan, you only need to communicate it with your employer. The plan is still handled by an investment house, but it is your employer that coordinates with them so that they can provide the plans to their employees. One drawback to this is that you will not be able to choose an investment house for yourself, so you must go with what your employer has chosen.

Regarding eligibility for a 401 (k) plan or a 403 (b) plan, you only need to be an employee for a profit-oriented organization who offers these plans. Currently, the rate for contributions is pegged at $18,000 per year and not more than that, which is the rate for those who are below 50 years of age. For ages 50 and older, you can invest more than that by adding another $6,000 to your contribution, so that you can invest to at most $24,000 each year.

As for taxation, a 401 (k) plan or a 403 (b) plan has a quite similar scheme with a Traditional IRA. While you are still paying your contributions, your payments will not be taxed and so you will have a relatively lower tax bill for the next year. You will only have to start paying taxes when you withdraw.

Just like a Traditional IRA, you can start withdrawing your money once you reach the age of 59.5 years. Again, remember that it is no longer tax-deductible once you withdraw. And like the Traditional IRA, it is compulsory that you must also withdraw from it when you are 70 years old if you have not yet done so. Early withdrawal is also allowed for a 401 (k) plan or a 403 (b) plan. But just like a Traditional IRA, there is a 10% penalty tax added for each withdrawal, on top of the regular tax.

3. Start investing.

You might think that having the plans above is enough to fund you throughout the rest of your retirement, but retirement experts suggest that you do not rely on these plans too much. This is because plans like these still have a few risks and drawbacks attached to them. For example, your withdrawals are still taxed despite whatever retirement plan you have. In addition, there is always the risk that your company will end up doing badly, even perhaps to a point of bankruptcy, which will surely affect your whole retirement savings. "Diversifying" your investments is one key to be more secure in the future.

For a good long-term solution, it is important that you spread your money into different investments. However, you cannot just dive into whatever investment you can find. You will need to make careful decisions on what and where to invest in since there are investments that may be attractive at first glance but are not appropriate in your condition as a future retiree. The suggested investment options that can offer you security would be bond funds, stock mutual funds, and money market funds. These are better options to put your money in since they grow faster than inflation rates and have relatively lower fees compared to other investments.

On the other hand, the retirement options to avoid include the following: life insurances, individual stocks and bonds, precious metals like gold and silver, annuities, certificate of deposit/time deposits, and the like. It is unwise to invest in them as they have higher risks and high costs. They are too impractical if you are thinking long term.

4. **Project your retirement savings and expenses, and then compare them.**

Once you have considered all your financial sources and chosen a plan and other investments, you can now compute for your future savings. While the result may just be an estimate, this will still allow you to make a good comparison.

To compute for your potential retirement savings, you can use an online savings calculator. This can help you compute what you will receive when you retire along with all the money that you saved. This will also tell you the probable result of your investment choices so that you can be flexible in your decisions. Savings calculators abound online, so it will be easy for you to find one.

Now, after you compute for your projected savings, you then need to compute for your projected expenses. List down what might be possible sources of expenses during your retirement. Most common retiree expenses would include mortgages, rent, debt from credit cards, tax payments, insurances, long term health care, loans, and other debts. Simply use basic computation for these, but do not forget to consider inflation rates. A quick look into the most recent government surveys can provide you with the figures that show how much an average retiree spends in a year.

Finally, think about what you plan to do during your retirement. Answer the following questions. Do you plan to go on a long vacation? What about traveling for most of the time? What are your hobbies? Do you plan on engaging in a new activity? How much will you spend on this? If you plan to retire overseas or move across the country, what are the costs of moving and settling here? For a list of things and activities that you may want to indulge in during your retirement, refer to Chapter 5 of this book.

After you have done all your estimations and computations, reflect on the resulting figure and decide whether you should stick with your plans or make appropriate changes. If you are still unsure, consult with your spouse on this, or a friend who has already retired to help you make better decisions.

CHAPTER 6

Things You Do After Retirement

After years and years of hard work, stressing yourself, and scrimping up on your savings, it would be wasteful to spend your retirement inside your house knitting sweaters or watching baseball games.

There are a lot of choices when it comes to hobbies or activities to engage in during your retirement. This chapter will introduce you to various activities and ideas that to enjoy during this time whether you will be spending your retirement alone or with your spouse and family.

Best Activities for Retirees

1. **Tour the world.** If you barely took time off for a vacation during your employment days, retirement is the best time to go to the places you have not gone to or countries that you have always dreamed of visiting. An intercontinental cruise tour would be good to try, too. You can also experience living in a country for a year or so and live in another country for the next. This is a good way to learn more about the country, like its culture and practices, not just its tourist spots and beaches.

2. **Tour your own country.** If foreign vacations and trips are out of consideration because of budget constraints, an intra-country tour would still give you enough satisfaction and relaxation. Besides, isn't it best to get to know your own country first before touring others? Aside from being budget-friendly, this enables you to reconnect with your roots and discover more about yourself. Whether you bring your

family with you or do it alone, either way, it would still be worth it. If you want, you can rent an RV or just buy your own motor home so that you can be safe and comfortable wherever you want to go.

3. **Relocate.** You might have been planning to move for a long time but because of time and financial limitations, you were not able to. Retirement is the time for you to do it. You can relocate to the country where you can live quietly and breath gulps of fresh air every day or, you can move to the city or suburbs where your needs are readily accessible.

4. **Give your house a makeover.** Retirement would also be a good time to shake things up a little in your house. Since it is a new beginning for you, might as well give your house a little makeover. It can be a major renovation or just minor touches. Either way, it will give you a sense of purpose and help you start afresh.

5. **Put up your own business.** With all the time that you have, you can readily put up your own business which you've always been interested in. Aside from finally becoming a

business owner and having an extra source of income, you are also able to do something that's stimulating. But don't overwork yourself. You can put up a simple one and just go with its flow. You don't have to put up a huge business to start with.

6. **Work part-time.** Another way of keeping yourself from boredom during retirement is by working part-time on a job that you have always wanted to do. That way, you will be working for a few hours a day and at the same time, interact with other people. The pay may be significantly lesser, but this can still help you augment your budget for small household expenses.

7. **Connect with people.** This would be a good time to enhance your social life again. Reconnect with your friends or make new ones by meeting fellow retirees in your town. You can also bond with your family more and go on outings, or try to visit relatives, especially ones whom you haven't in contact with for years. Another option would be to volunteer in babysitting your grandchildren or your neighbor's children.

8. **Share your knowledge.** As retirees, you surely have gained enough experience and knowledge on your respective fields. You can use this expertise to teach younger people. Mentoring can be one example. Your local community college might also be a good start, or you can volunteer your free services as an instructor in a local non-government organization or charity group. You can be active in government work, too, and contribute your wisdom for local public service.

9. **Give school another shot.** You may have had to quit school back then or you took a degree you were not fond of. In any case, retirement is the best time to be a student again, especially if you really want to learn more about the field you are interested in. This is one good way of keeping your brain active and healthy. If school is out of the question for you, you can try studying your interests on your own. There are many sources online or in the library for your perusal. Instead of reading, why not try writing a book or starting a blog? It's a good

way to keep you busy and make use of your know-how.

10. Try new things. If you want to learn new stuff, you do not necessarily have to go to school. Other endeavors like learning to play an instrument or learning a new language can easily be self-taught. There are many self-help books available that can guide you. Online sources are easily accessible, as well. You can start trying new hobbies, too, like photography, painting, fishing, sculpting, collecting, solving puzzles, and many more.

How about getting more active? You can play sports either for fun or for competition. Either way, staying active is good to keep your mind and body strong and healthy and ward off diseases that come with age.

Best Countries to Retire To

If ever you are open to settling in another country for your retirement, choosing the best country to retire to is important. Below is a full list of countries to live in or at least visit, as a retiree.

1. **Ecuador.** This country has consistently topped the list for retirement spots. Thousands of retirees have been traveling to Ecuador and enjoying their stay as retirees there. It is a good place to live in as real estate has good value and the cost of living there is low. In addition, its GDP has also been growing at a steady the past years, painting a good future for the economic situation in the country. Infrastructure and services in the country are also well commended.

2. **Panama.** The country has also been surrounded by hype made by overseas retirees. Like Ecuador, Panama has also experienced a surge in foreign visitors, mostly retirees who wish to live there. One major aspect that makes Panama a very attractive retirement destination is the special visa that the Panama government offers to its retirees, local or not. Advantages include 30% discount on public transportation like boats, buses, and train fares, 25% discount on air travel, 50% discount on leisure and entertainment activities like theaters, movies, sports events, concerts and more, up to 50% discount on

hotel accommodations, 15% discount on medical bills, and 25% discount on electric bills. Visa holders will also receive at least $1,000 per month as pension.

3. **Mexico.** This country has consistently been on the top list of retirement sites. One good thing about Mexico is its proximity to the country, making your move less of a hassle. Mexico is a very colorful country rife with culture and beauty. Another thing that also attracts retirees to Mexico is its strong internet connection and astounding cellular coverage, perfect for keeping in touch with your loved ones back home. The country is very flexible when it comes to choosing a retirement environment since it has it all— from beachfront to mountain regions, modern metropolis, and farms. The real estate industry is also booming and very prolific, along with the affordable cost of living. You can buy a lot with your $50 there compared to when you are in your own country. Health care is also very cheap here but still has good quality.

4. **Malaysia.** Malaysia is the only Asian country to reach the top 5 on the retirement

list and there is a good reason for it. The Malaysian economy is very consistent and strong and the quality of life in the country is very good, whether you are a citizen or foreign retiree. Rental for premium real estate is also very affordable here, as well as the basic commodities. If you are thinking of constantly visiting your relatives and friends back home, the country also has very cheap flights offered by several international airlines. Getting around is not a problem here, too, with very smooth roads and efficient public transportation system. If you are worried about healthcare, don't be. The quality of healthcare here in Malaysia is comparable to that in first world countries but with significantly more affordable rates.

5. **Spain.** If you want to spend your retirement in Europe, Spain is the perfect place for you. It is considered the most affordable retirement destination cn the continent. Many retirees have moved to Spain due to its retained unique history and vibrant culture while keeping up with technology and infrastructure advancements. Not only that,

the cost of living is cheaper here than any other European country, but it has a high standard of living. Healthcare here is renowned around the world for its great value, while public services like transportation, internet, and cellular coverage are very efficient. Spain is also a great choice if you are not fond of cold weather. The warm climate of Spain has made it very popular for retirees from colder countries who find the chill aggravating their health condition.

Conclusion

It is my sincere wish that you have enjoyed reading this book. I hope that you have learned a lot about retirement and how to live comfortably and happily after that. May you be enlightened about its benefits, the different options that you can make, the steps on how to prepare for it, and the activities that you can enjoy when you finally retire.

Retirement is a serious matter. You cannot just simply say, "At that age, I will retire." It is more complicated than that, and as such, it needs more careful planning. You can be faced with different options that you should look into before choosing the right kind of retirement plan for you.

Now, all you must do is to start planning for your future especially when you think that it is about time for you to retire. It may take some time before you could come up with a good plan, but know that it will be all worth it.

Again, thank you for purchasing this book and may you have a happy retirement!

www.ingramcontent.com/pod-product-compliance
Lightning Source LLC
Chambersburg PA
CBHW070933180526
45168CB00003B/1065